Library Technology
REPORTS
Expert Guides to Library Systems and Services

Librarians' Assessments of WITHDRAWN Automation Systems

Survey Results, 2007–2010

Marshall Breeding and Andromeda Yelton

ALA TechSource
alatechsource.org

American Library Association

Library Technology
R E P O R T S

ALA TechSource purchases fund advocacy, awareness, and accreditation programs for library professionals worldwide.

Volume 47, Number 4

Librarians' Assessments of Automation Systems: Survey Results, 2007–2010

ISBN: 978-0-8389-5832-2

American Library Association

50 East Huron St.
Chicago, IL 60611-2795 USA
alatechsource.org
800-545-2433, ext. 4299
312-944-6780
312-280-5275 (fax)

Advertising Representative

Brian Searles, Ad Sales Manager
ALA Publishing Dept.
bsearles@ala.org
312-280-5282
1-800-545-2433, ext. 5282

Editor

Dan Freeman
dfreeman@ala.org
312-280-5413

Copy Editor

Judith Lauber

Editorial Assistant

Megan O'Neill
moneill@ala.org
800-545-2433, ext. 3244
312-280-5275 (fax)

Production and Design

Tim Clifford, Production Editor
Karen Sheets de Gracia, Manager of Design and Composition

Library Technology Reports (ISSN 0024-2586) is published eight times a year (January, March, April, June, July, September, October, and December) by American Library Association, 50 E. Huron St., Chicago, IL 60611. It is managed by ALA TechSource, a unit of the publishing department of ALA. Periodical postage paid at Chicago, Illinois, and at additional mailing offices. POSTMASTER: Send address changes to Library Technology Reports, 50 E. Huron St., Chicago, IL 60611.

ALA TechSource
alatechsource.org

About the Authors

Marshall Breeding, director for innovative technology and research for the Vanderbilt University Library, is also a speaker, writer, and consultant. He is the creator and editor of Library Technology Guides (www.librarytechnology.org), a columnist for *Computers in Libraries*, editor of *Smart Libraries*, and has authored the annual "Automation Marketplace" published by *Library Journal* since 2002. He has authored nine issues of ALA's *Library Technology Reports*, and has written many other articles and book chapters. Marshall has edited or authored six books. He regularly teaches workshops and gives presentations internationally at library conferences.

Andromeda Yelton is a member of the founding team at Gluejar. She is a 2010 Simmons GSLIS graduate interested in the intersection of people, technology, and information. Yelton is a 2011 ALA Emerging Leader and a 2010 winner of the LITA/Ex Libris Student Writing Award.

Abstract

This report elaborates on the results of Marshall Breeding's 2010 survey of libraries' satisfaction with their automation products, and examines trends that have emerged over the four years the survey has been conducted. Chapter 1 details the survey methodology and limits, and outlines its findings. Chapter 2 delves into respondents' comments to explore the themes that may be motivating libraries' ratings of their systems. These include concerns about cost, relationships with consortia, and varying expectations for functionality. Libraries' mixed feelings on open source options are also discussed.

Chapter 3 then examines the numerical data, looking at satisfaction for major ILS products and vendors. Different library types (public and academic) and sizes are compared. Respondents' comments provide some context for these ratings. Chapter 3 also examines trends in satisfaction and interest in open source over time; satisfaction is flat or slightly increasing, whereas the picture for open source is complicated. Finally, by comparing 2007 and 2010 data, Chapter 3 finds that libraries' vendor loyalty ratings do indicate the future likelihood of migration.

Chapter 4 examines in depth a few major ILS vendors, which span a range of library types and satisfaction ratings, and speculates on the reasons for these ratings.

Subscriptions
alatechsource.org/subscribe

Contents

About the Perceptions Survey

Abstract

Chapter 1 details the methodology of the Perceptions survey and notes its limits; readers are encouraged not to base decisions solely on the content of this report. Chapter 1 also outlines the findings of the remaining chapters.

For the last four years, Marshall Breeding has conducted an online survey to measure satisfaction with multiple aspects of the automation products used by libraries. The results of the four editions of the survey data, along with brief interpretive narratives, have been published on Library Technology Guides. This issue of *Library Technology Reports* will take a deeper look at the survey data, including an expansion of findings based on the 2010 iteration, an examination of trends seen across the four years, and additional analysis not previously published. For this report, the survey data have been extended with additional fields that provide the opportunity to separate the findings into categories that show some interesting trends not otherwise apparent.

Goals of the Survey

Why conduct this survey? In this time of tight budgets where libraries face difficult decisions regarding how to invest their technology resources, it's helpful to have data regarding how libraries perceive the quality of their automation systems and the companies that support them. This report, based on survey responses from more than two thousand libraries, aims to give some measure of how libraries perceive their current environment and to probe their inclinations for the future, as well as investigating trends that have emerged over the four years of the Perceptions survey.

Library Technology Guides
www.librarytechnology.org

Some libraries may refer to the results of this survey as they formulate technology strategies or even consider specific products. Libraries are urged not to base any decision solely on this report. While it reflects the responses of a large number of libraries using these products, this survey serves best as an instrument to guide what questions a library might bring up in its considerations. We caution libraries not to make premature conclusions based on subjective responses. Especially for libraries with more complex needs, it's unrealistic to expect satisfaction scores at the very top of the rankings. Large and complex libraries exercise all aspects of an automation system and at any given time may have outstanding issues that would naturally result in survey responses short of the highest marks.

How the Data Were Collected

The survey instrument included six numeric ratings, three yes/no responses, three short response fields, and a text field for general comments. The numeric rating fields allow responses from 0 through 9. Each scale was labeled to indicate the meaning of the numeric selection.

Five of the numeric questions probe at the level of satisfaction with and loyalty to the company or organization that provides its current automation system:

- How satisfied is the library with your current **Integrated Library System?**
- How satisfied is the library overall with the **company** from which you purchased your current ILS?

- How satisfied is this library with this company's **customer support** services?
- Has the **customer support** for your ILS gotten better or gotten worse in the last year?
- Would your library consider working with this company again if your library were to migrate to a new ILS in the future?

One yes/no question asks whether the library is considering migrating to a new ILS and a fill-in text field provides the opportunity to provide specific systems under consideration. Another yes/no question asks whether the automation system currently in use was installed on schedule and according to the terms of the contract.

Given the recent interest in new search interfaces, a third yes/no question asks, "Is this library currently considering acquiring a **discovery interface** or **Next-generation catalog** for its collection that is separate from the ILS?" and provides a fill-in form to indicate products under consideration.

The survey includes two questions that aim to gauge interest in open source integrated library systems, a numerical rating that asks "How likely is it that this library would consider implementing an open source ILS?" and a fill-in text field for indicating products under consideration.

The survey concludes with a text box inviting comments. A copy of the survey may be viewed online. (This version of the survey does not accept or record response data.)

In order to correlate the responses with particular automation systems and companies, the survey links to

Library Automation Survey
www.librarytechnology.org/lwc
-automation-survey-2010.pl

entries in the lib-web-cats directory of libraries. Each entry in lib-web-cats indicates the automation system currently in use as well as data on the type of library, location, collection size, and other factors that might be of interest. In order to fill out the survey, responders first had to find their library in lib-web-cats and then press a button that launched the response form. Some potential respondents indicated that they found this process complex.

The link between the lib-web-cats entry and the survey automatically populated fields for the library name and current automation system and provided access to other data elements about the library as needed. The report on survey response demographics, for example, relies on data from lib-web-cats.

A number of methods were used to solicit responses to the survey. E-mail messages were sent to library-oriented mailing lists such as WEB4LIB, PUBLIB, and

lib-web-cats Directory
www.librarytechnology.org/libwebcats

NGC4LIB. Invitational messages were also sent to many lists for specific automation systems and companies. Where contact information was available in lib-web-cats, an automated script produced e-mail messages with a direct link to the survey response form for that library.

The survey limited responses to one per library, though it allowed responses from multiple branches or facilities associated with a system. This restriction was imposed as an attempt to sway the respondents to reflect the broad perceptions of their institution rather than their personal opinions.

The survey instrument was created using the same infrastructure as the Library Technology Guides website—a custom interface written in Perl using MySQL to store the data, with ODBC as the connection layer. Access to the raw responses is controlled through a user name and password available only to the author. Scripts allow public access to the survey results in a way that does not expose individual responses.

In order to provide access to the comments without violating the stated agreement not to attribute individual responses to any given institution or individual, an additional field was created for edited comments. This field was manually populated with text selected from the comment text provided by the respondent. Any information that might identify the individual or library was edited out, with an ellipsis indicating the removed text. Comments that only explained a response or described the circumstances of the library were not transferred to the edited comments field.

Caveats and Limitations of the Survey Data

There are several limitations to keep in mind while analyzing the survey data.

First, although the survey is quite large (at 2,000 + libraries), it is by no means comprehensive. There are well over 57,000 libraries in lib-web-cats, which itself represents only a portion of the total libraries worldwide, and methods used do not ensure that the survey respondents are a random or representative sample. For example, Innovative customers had a relatively high response rate, giving Millennium prominence in the survey out of proportion to its market share. Survey responses, though including many international libraries, skew heavily toward North America; nearly 1,700 of the respondents are from libraries in the United States. Similarly, although many library types are represented, public and academic libraries alone comprise more than 1,700 of the responses. Therefore other demographics may be underrepresented.

Second, it cannot be guaranteed that respondents' choices fully represented the libraries' views. Though survey instructions requested that respondents speak for their institutions, the survey cannot ensure this. In addition, respondents sometimes commented that they did not have direct contact with their support vendors or direct influence over their library automation choices because those were handled through a central IT office or consortially. It is not clear how this impacts their satisfaction ratings.

Third, libraries do not consistently fill out the survey from year to year. While comparing results over time can reveal broad trends, it is not necessarily possible to track how individual libraries' opinions changed, and comparisons between different years are not apples-to-apples.

Basic Findings of the Data

Because the survey included both numeric data and a comment field, we were able both to gauge overall satisfaction with various products and services and to speculate on the reasons behind those ratings.

In chapter 2, we discuss issues frequently raised in the comments, which included cost, consortia, open source software, and ILS functionality. Comments on cost, of course, were almost universally negative, reflecting libraries' concerns about limited budgets and the increasing price of software. Many libraries feel that they pay too much for their automation systems. Libraries have mixed feelings on consortia, appreciating the savings and shared expertise they offer but sometimes feeling that their individual needs are lost in the mix. They also complain about not having a direct voice in software selection and support.

The survey was designed to probe perceptions regarding open source library automation systems, with both a numeric indicator and a corresponding comment. About 10 percent of libraries responding had already implemented open source systems; others appeared drawn to such systems as a potential low-cost alternative, though still others questioned whether the total cost of ownership would truly yield savings. Many libraries expressed concern, however, about the functionality and maturity of open source products or the expertise needed to maintain them and do not think they are viable alternatives at this time. It is unclear what these concerns will mean for the future.

Comments on ILS functionality also varied tremendously. Some libraries expressed pleasure at the modern features of their ILS while others said it was outdated and clunky—even when they used the same software. Some libraries are doing local development or customization which places specific technical demands on the ILS, but many do not have the in-house expertise to do this. Almost a quarter of respondents are looking for discovery layers or other next-generation catalog features—in some cases to replace an existing product of that type, in others as a first system; however, comments rarely go into depth on libraries' opinions of these products.

Although libraries' demands on ILS functionality varied, there was general agreement that ILSes should be modern, fast, and easy to use. There was also some interest in the potential simplicity and cost savings of cloud solutions.

In chapter 3, we move on to the numerical ratings for ILS, company, and customer support satisfaction and examine trends by size and type of library. Although there are some products used in a wide variety of market niches, in general larger and smaller libraries gravitate toward different ILSes. Smaller libraries use a wider variety of ILSes than larger ones and tend to be more satisfied with them; Apollo, OPALS, and Polaris scored particularly well. Similarly, library type (public or academic) affects both the ILSes used and the ratings. While Millennium, Horizon, and Symphony are widely used in both types of library, public libraries also commonly use Polaris and Library•Solution, whereas academic libraries use Voyager and Aleph. Public libraries are somewhat more satisfied with their software, vendors, and support than academic libraries; this is true even for larger libraries, and even when comparing the same ILS. Libraries' satisfaction with their software has remained roughly constant or perhaps, in some cases, increased slightly over the four years of the Perceptions survey, while average satisfaction with companies and customer support has generally increased, along with libraries' loyalty to their current vendor. Satisfied libraries tend to cite the quality of support and say that their vendors listen to them, whereas reasons for dissatisfaction vary, including concerns over software functionality, support quality, and vendors' business direction.

We also examine interest in open source in 2010 and over time and find a complicated picture. Although the most common level of interest in open source is 0, the next most common is 9. This polarization appears to have increased over time, with more libraries indicating extreme scores and fewer at most scores between 1 and 8. The growth in high interest can be partly, but not entirely, accounted for by open source adopters, who almost always indicate very high levels of interest in open source. Comments indicate interest in the potential affordability and flexibility of open source software, but concerns about its functionality and maturity and about a lack of in-house technical expertise. It is not clear what this means for future trends. Historically highly interested libraries have been much more likely to adopt open source ILSes, so the growth in that category may indicate future adoptions; on the other hand, it may be that libraries that are interested but have not yet migrated to such products do not feel they are viable options at present. Either way, there are far more libraries averse to open source than interested in it.

Also in chapter 3, we examine the relationship between libraries' stated loyalty and whether they are shopping for a new ILS. Indeed, low-loyalty libraries are much more likely than high-loyalty ones to be in the market for a new ILS. Low-loyalty ones are also much more likely to be considering an open source candidate, whereas high-loyalty libraries that are nonetheless seeking a new ILS are likely to be looking at another product line from the same company. In comparing 2007 Perceptions survey data to migration data in lib-web-cats, we find that libraries which indicated that they are shopping are, indeed, much more likely to have migrated; therefore, company loyalty likely impacts the chance of migration.

Finally, because we now have four years of Perceptions survey data, we look for trends over time. We find that average satisfaction with ILSes, companies, and customer support has remained roughly constant, with perhaps a slight upward trend in some scores for some products. Nonetheless, company loyalty has increased. It is not clear why this is. Perhaps economic concerns make migrations less likely, so libraries are necessarily loyal to their current vendors, or perhaps libraries that formerly had low loyalty have switched vendors.

In chapter 4, we look closely at specific vendors (Polaris, Apollo, SirsiDynix, Millennium, and several Koha support strategies), which span a range of library types and satisfaction ratings. By examining the comments, we look for the reasons behind those ratings.

Analyzing Comments for Themes

Abstract

Chapter 2 examines themes that commonly arose in the comments: cost; the benefits and drawbacks of consortial membership; ILS functionality; customer support; and open source software. While comments on cost are almost universally negative, the other topics reflect a range of opinions. Librarians want mature, intuitive software with responsive vendors. They disagree on whether their current products, or open source alternatives, provide this.

We categorized the comments from the free text field to look for hot-button issues. Popular areas of interest included costs; consortia; open source (no doubt partly because other survey questions directly addressed this); ILS functionality; and customer support. Libraries commenting on their support typically either loved it or hated it, and this issue will be addressed in more depth and in the context of specific vendors in chapter 4. The other themes will be addressed here.

Costs

A very large number of comments centered on the costs involved with annual maintenance and support. Not only were the costs perceived as high, but the annual increases were burdensome. Many libraries noted that given budget pressures, current levels of cost for maintenance were not sustainable. A few were satisfied with their ILS and support, but still considering migration due to cost concerns. Some knew they were making tradeoffs in terms of functionality to reach a good price point, but were satisfied with the overall package. For many, however, the costs,

in terms of both funds for a new system and the personnel efforts required, precluded change and forced continuation of the status quo despite some degree of dissatisfaction.

Consortia

Commenters addressed both the benefits and the drawbacks of consortia membership.

On the positive side, many libraries make use of an automation system provided through a consortium. This arrangement allows them to benefit from the use of a full-featured system, at a cost lower than they would pay individually, and to rely on technical support provided through the consortium. Several comments indicated that the consortium made it possible to use a system they otherwise couldn't afford or to benefit from technical expertise they did not have in house. Other libraries not in consortia expressed a hope that they could find partners that would allow them to experience these benefits.

However, some libraries sharing an ILS though a consortium expressed concerns regarding the choice of system imposed by the consortium, constraints in functionality, and issues in the way that consortium delivered services. These libraries may have been dissatisfied with the choice of ILS—in some cases thinking it was a step backward from their previous automation system—but they felt powerless to effect change. Many libraries involved with consortia noted that they were unable to evaluate the performance of their ILS vendor or provide feedback because their support was mediated through the consortium. This in turn may make it difficult for vendors to be appropriately responsive to users' needs.

Library Technology Reports alatechsource.org May/June 2011

Open Source

Open source ILSes have been a prominent topic of discussion in recent years, and the survey has specifically addressed this since its inception by asking about level of interest in open source products and specific products under consideration. While some pockets of interest in open source ILS software surface, the survey does not reveal widespread interest outside the ranks of libraries already invested in one of these systems. Libraries' comments on this issue are diverse and the overall picture is complicated. (See also the section on interest in open source in chapter 3.)

Just over 10 percent of survey respondents currently operate open source ILS products, with generally moderate to high satisfaction scores. Open source was among the most prominent topics in the comments among both adopters and nonadopters (possibly because the survey specifically asked about it); despite the relatively high satisfaction of the adopters, most of the comments by nonadopters expressed concern.

Among libraries running proprietary systems, many felt that the open source products lacked the functionality and maturity they required; others noted that they did not have the in-house technical expertise they anticipated would be necessary to implement open source automation systems. It's clear that many libraries continue to believe that the use of open source software requires local programming capabilities and may not be aware of the fully managed options available through specialized support and hosting companies.

Some functionality concerns were quite specific. One library "is using many self-check machines (3M), and we need a ILS with SIP2 protocol support." Another needs "a robust Spanish interface, support for floating collections and an acquisitions module"; another echoed the concern about the "lack of an integrated acquisitions module." One said, quite simply, "The last time our systems administrator tried to install Koha, it didn't work." However, the majority of these comments were phrased in general terms, such as "We don't feel the open source ILS options are mature enough, yet." Functionality, maturity, and viability were the recurring ideas in this category.

The availability and cost of support and the presence or absence of in-house expertise were also frequent themes. For example, "We do not have the resources (staff, skill-set) to even think about open source products, especially if we had to go it alone, much as we might like to." This succinctly addresses three common themes: first, that organizations with no immediate likelihood of migration to open source are still interested in it; second, that lack of technical expertise is a significant barrier to ILS adoption; and third, that some libraries see consortial help as necessary to adopt such products.

It is important to note that these concerns were expressed in both positive and negative terms. Some libraries dismissed open source ILSes as a viable option; others said that they will be interested in open source once these concerns are addressed; and still others, which have adopted open source products, noted that the availability of in-house or consortial expertise was a key factor in their decision.

Cost was also an important theme in comments, and again for mixed reasons. Some libraries are interested in open source specifically, if not solely, to save money, citing the high cost of proprietary systems. Others have found that the hosting or development costs of open source do not compete favorably with the licensing and support costs of their existing proprietary systems. Indeed, while some libraries have found open source to be cheaper, others have found it more expensive.

The dominant theme in libraries' comments on open source cost, however, was uncertainty. One library said, "We do understand open source does not mean free but don't have a good understanding of the potential cost . . ."; another echoed this with "There is interest in open source tools, believing they would be a panacea to all woes, but a lack of real knowledge about the maturity of such products and the actual costs of implementation and operation." For at least one library, this uncertainty is definitive: "In these financially challenging times, libraries would be prudent to acquire stable systems with known costs, rather than rolling the dice and hoping that 'open source' will be a panacea for their automation needs."

Finally, one library foreshadowed possible trends with a heartfelt plea: "Clear directions for complex procedures . . . do not exist for setting up either system and so they seem at present to be restricted to those with database coding skills. Please fix this, open developers! We want to use your systems!" In other words, while the vast majority of libraries right now are invested in proprietary solutions, they are not necessarily committed. Technological, philosophical, or financial interests sometimes favor open source adoption. If a full-featured system with turnkey or cloud simplicity emerged, it could induce a tipping point in the market.

Data, Software Architecture, and Functionality

Interest in software design and function was also a common theme in the comments, ranging from front-end functionality and usability to specific, technical software architecture concerns.

Far and away the major theme in this category was interest in, or use of, discovery layers and other new-generation catalog features. (Note that, although the comments field was unrestricted, two of the survey

Library Technology Reports alatechsource.org May/June 2011

questions asked about interest in such products.) Commenters represented libraries with existing discovery systems; those in the process of investigating or acquiring such systems; and those that are interested, but cannot presently afford to implement them. Their comments rarely went in depth on libraries' opinions of these products. The percentage of libraries in the sample considering acquiring such systems has remained roughly constant, at 20–25%, since 2007; some of these are looking for a first system, while others are commenting on—or looking to replace—an existing system. The survey does not permit reliable statistics on how many libraries have already implemented such a system.

The next most common theme was usability. Some libraries were dissatisfied with their product's ease of use; for instance, "Far too many clicks, drop down bars, and changing of default settings are required to perform simple searches" or "If you look up a patron it's in one 'wizard' then if they check something out, it's another 'wizard' to pay a fine is another, to renew items another. Everything is in a separate place." One summarized it thus: "With the world used to speed and the intuitiveness of Google or Amazon.com this software seems clunky and outdated."

Perhaps in line with this interest in modern, streamlined features, the comments reflected a certain interest in cloud computing and hosted solutions. Although few comments went into depth on these interests, those that did suggested that tech support and cost savings were potential benefits of moving to the cloud.

Finally, there were comments expressing interest in the fine details of software functionality. Around half of these praised, or wanted, the ability to customize their product (for example, its look and feel, or its reporting options). The other half reflected specific technical interests: for instance, desire for (and use of) exposed application programming interfaces and integrability with third-party modules.

The overall message is that librarians want their software to be intuitive, capable, and modern. A small but articulate minority care about the details of architecture and function; they want to be able to make their ILS work for local needs.

Breaking Down the Data

Abstract

Chapter 3 examines differences in ILS satisfaction by library type (public vs. academic) and size. Satisfied libraries praise quality customer service; dissatisfied ones mention a variety of issues, including business direction, ILS functionality, customer service problems, and cost. Chapter 3 also examines trends over time for both satisfaction and interest in open source, and speculates on reasons behind these trends. Finally, it examines the relationship between company loyalty and future migration.

ILS Satisfaction

As mentioned in chapter 2, a few products—notably Apollo and OPALS—received exceptionally high satisfaction ratings. These products typically serve small libraries; therefore both the products and the libraries may not be reflective of trends for other types of libraries. Through the linkages to lib-web-cats, it's possible to associate survey responses with additional data elements to bring in factors such as library type or size of collection. We were also able, by using data from lib-web-cats, to correlate library collection size for most, although not all, of the libraries in the survey. This let us examine ILS and customer support satisfaction for three sizes of library—smaller, larger, and very large—and two types—public and academic. There were not enough respondents from other library types in the survey to permit meaningful comparisons.

One caveat: collection size is self-reported, and libraries may use different metrics; for instance, they may make different choices about how to count electronic content. Therefore the breakdown by library size should be taken as a broad approximation.

When segregating the survey data by the size of the library, in this case determined by those with collections over 50,000 volumes, much more interesting results are revealed than from the total aggregate data. This view of the data filters out the ultrapositive responses submitted primarily by small libraries, providing a more fair comparison of those companies and products that serve all but the smallest libraries. Removing the smallest libraries, and the 347 for which collection size could not be determined, leaves 1,043 out of the 2,102 total survey responses (figure 1). Note also that only products with at least 20 active sites generate discrete entries in the summary tables.

In this view of the data filtering out smaller libraries, Polaris stands out as the ILS with the most positive ratings, with an average of 7.84. Millennium ranks second with 7.19. A middle group of products (Library•Solution, Aleph, and Evergreen) all rank between 6.4 and 6.75. Voyager, Symphony, and Horizon received similar ratings around 5.9.

By looking at the comments, we can see some of the reasons behind these ratings. While top-ranking Polaris has usability concerns for some customers, many agree that "customer support is beyond excellent," including increased responsiveness over the past year. Libraries feel that "they really listen to our issues, thoughts, and suggestions"; for example, "via the Polaris Users Group enhancement process." One library feels that "The customer service is unparalleled. I would not say that I would stand on a street corner in a clown suit to sell it, but it's close." Notably, few of these comments are about the software itself; rather, they note the libraries' exceedingly positive relationship with their vendor, which seems to translate into satisfaction with the product.

How satisfied is the library with your current Integrated Library System (ILS)? (collection size > 50,000)																
Company	Responses	Response Distribution										Satisfaction Score			
		0	1	2	3	4	5	6	7	8	9	Mode	Mean	Median	Std Dev
Polaris	67			1	2	1	1	1	12	23	26	9	7.84	8	0.86
Millennium	264	1	2	1	1	8	16	26	84	89	36	8	7.19	7	0.55
Library·Solution	51			1	3	5	4	4	9	19	6	8	6.75	7	1.12
ALEPH 500	86		1	1	4	2	10	17	33	15	3	7	6.43	7	0.97
Evergreen	20			1		1	3	4	7	2	2	7	6.40	7	1.57
Voyager	93			4	3	7	18	23	26	11	1	7	5.94	6	0.62
Symphony (Unicorn)	163	2	4	7	11	12	22	26	40	31	8	7	5.92	6	0.55
Horizon	134	1	1	7	9	16	16	22	33	21	8	7	5.89	6	0.60
All Responses	1,043	6	9	25	39	59	105	139	296	250	115	7	6.59	7	0.22

Note: Number of responses required for product to be included in the analysis = 20.

Figure 1
ILS satisfaction in larger libraries.

As for Millennium, a common theme seems to be "We are happy with III/Millennium except for the cost." Indeed, while satisfaction ratings are generally high—and there is a great deal of interest in Innovative's discovery interface, Encore—many comments are negative. Libraries express concern about maintenance costs and about having to pay individually for new features, including "basic functionality (faceted browsing, spell check etc) that is part of other companies' standard web catalogs, but must be purchased from III."

Reasons for dissatisfaction with the lower-ranked products vary. Some Horizon customers expressed concern that closures and consolidations of SirsiDynix offices resulted in important institutional knowledge being lost, with a corresponding decline in customer service. They also wonder what their upgrade path will be as SirsiDynix shifts its focus to Symphony. Symphony libraries speak somewhat more positively of customer support, although they note that quality varies. Many expressed concern regarding high maintenance costs.

Comments on Voyager are more likely to center on technical issues. While some customers are concerned that the product may be outdated and underdeveloped, others speak well of the technical support resources available. Voyager is also praised for participating in the open source community and exposing APIs.

It seems that, to paraphrase Tolstoy, happy libraries are all alike, in their satisfaction with customer service; every unhappy library is unhappy in its own way. Although cost is a major concern for users of many different ILS products (including those who are otherwise satisfied), unhappy libraries also wonder about companies' strategies for their product lines; usability, functionality, and feature development; and customer service, especially responsiveness.

Indeed, one key theme to emerge from the comments was listening. (This will be treated more fully in chapter 4.) Libraries that are satisfied with their ILS frequently commended their vendors for listening to them in a caring, responsive way. Libraries that are dissatisfied mentioned unresponsive customer service personnel and companies that did not act on bug reports or feature requests, which one profoundly dissatisfied library summarized with, "It would be nice to have vendors listen to our needs for a change."

Finally, recall that many libraries, while they did submit ratings, noted that they could not fully evaluate their satisfaction with the company because their consortium (or, in some cases, their IT department) is the point of contact for service issues. These libraries do not have a direct way to communicate their feature requests or other needs to their vendors and do not have direct experience of their customer service. It is not clear what their ratings indicate, nor can they be filtered out of the data.

We can also disaggregate the data for larger libraries by library type to see if trends differ. Among these libraries, only academic and public library types had enough responses to examine (see figures 2 and 3). Both academic and larger public libraries show generally high satisfaction with Millennium, driving its second place overall satisfaction ranking among larger public libraries and top place with academics. And both types of library are less happy with the two SirsiDynix products, Horizon and Symphony.

However, public and academic libraries diverge in which ILSes they use. While some systems such as Millennium, Horizon, and Symphony find use across library types, ALEPH 500 and Voyager target academic and research libraries, while Polaris and Library·Solution appeal more to public libraries.

How satisfied is the library with your current Integrated Library System (ILS)? (collection size > 50,000, public libraries)					
Company	Responses	Response Distribution			
		0	1	2	3
Polaris	60				1
Millennium	101			1	
Library·Solution	40				3
Horizon	101	1		5	6
Symphony (Unicorn)	76	1	1	6	7
All Responses	493	2	2	15	19

Note: Number of responses required for product to be included in the analysis = 20.

How satisfied is the library with your current Integrated Library System (ILS)? (collection size > 50,000, academic libraries)					
Company	Responses	Response Distribution			
		0	1	2	3
Millennium	127		2	1	
ALEPH 500	68			1	5
Voyager	85			2	3
Symphony (Unicorn)	72		4	1	3
Horizon	23		1	2	2
All Responses	469	2	7	13	17

Note: Number of responses required for product to be included in the analysis = 20.

Figure 2
ILS satisfaction in larger public libraries.

Figure 3
ILS satisfaction in larger academic libraries.

While some implement these systems outside their target markets, the numbers don't reach the thresholds to be included in the tables. For example, ALEPH 500 and Voyager, both strongly represented in the academic sample, are scarcely used in the public library world (neither meets the threshold of 20 sites required for inclusion here). Similarly, Polaris and Library·Solution have only a handful of academic sites. This sheds light on two aspects of the overall ranking in figure 1.

First, the tiers of rankings correspond roughly to library type. Number 1 Polaris and number 3 Library·Solution are both public library ILSes; number 4 ALEPH 500 and number 6 Voyager are both academic library products.

Evergreen, an open source ILS used primarily by public library consortia, earned moderate ratings (6.40) in the view of the data showing only larger libraries. However, Evergreen does not have enough installed sites in these libraries to be included in figure 2.

Second, academic libraries are simply less satisfied than public libraries overall. Public libraries are more satisfied than academics with all three of the ILSes (Millennium, Symphony, and Horizon) in common use in both library types. They are more likely to be highly satisfied regardless of product; note the mode of 8 for public libraries versus 7 for academic libraries.

The survey does not specifically address the reasons why public libraries may have generally higher levels of satisfaction than their academic counterparts. We speculate that the traditional automation systems in use today covered by the survey don't fare as well with the more complex collections of academic libraries and their increased orientation toward electronic resources. Public libraries continue to rely on their automation systems handling their physical collections, which these systems continue to do quite well.

When we turn our attention again to the 719 smaller libraries (collection size under 50,000) in the survey, we find they differ from larger libraries in several ways (figure 4). First, they are more likely to be extremely satisfied with their products. As noted above, high marks for Apollo and OPALS are part of this picture. However, even when comparing satisfaction levels with the same product, smaller libraries tend to be happier than larger ones. Note the ratings for Library·Solution (mean of 7.24 for smaller libraries versus 6.75 for larger ones), Horizon (6.85 versus 5.89), and Symphony (6.18 versus 5.92). Millennium (6.79 versus 7.19) is an exception to this trend, but its ratings among smaller libraries still indicate moderately high satisfaction.

One aspect of the very high satisfaction seen in small libraries lies in automation products that offer the right level of functionality for their needs. These libraries may feel overwhelmed by the complexity of some of the higher-end products, especially Millennium. Fully managed and hosted products, such as Apollo and OPALS, remove much of the burden of automation from these libraries, offering an ample number of features through a Web-based system with no need to manage software on local servers or workstations. Many of the libraries implementing Apollo have migrated from long-outdated systems such as Winnebago Spectrum, Athena, InfoCentre, or Circulation Plus or may have automated for the first time. These right-sized solutions in tandem with high quality and personalized support may underlie the superlative perceptions of these libraries.

Other smaller libraries also appreciated other fully hosted systems, though at slightly lower levels, such as Koha supported by ByWater Solutions (7.81) and AGent VERSO from Auto-Graphics (7.28). Library·Solution from the Library Corporation also fared well with smaller libraries (7.24). It's no surprise that Winnebago

How satisfied is the library with your current Integrated Library System (ILS)? (collection size < 50,000)															
Company	Responses	Response Distribution										Satisfaction Score			
		0	1	2	3	4	5	6	7	8	9	Mode	Mean	Median	Std Dev
Apollo	69							1	4	12	52	9	8.67	9	1.08
OPALS	89						1	1	10	15	62	9	8.53	9	0.95
Koha—ByWater Solutions	21						1	1	7	4	8	9	7.81	8	1.53
AGent VERSO	57				1	1	2	6	26	9	12	7	7.28	7	1.19
Library Solution	37				4		2	3	7	10	11	9	7.24	8	1.48
Circulation Plus	21				1	2	2	1	7	3	5	7	6.90	7	1.75
Atriuum	20	1			1		1	2	5	7	3	8	6.90	8	1.79
Horizon	27					2	2	7	7	5	4	6	6.85	7	1.15
Millennium	38			2	1	1	1	4	18	7	4	7	6.79	7	0.81
Destiny	20		1	1	1	1	2	2	1	9	2	8	6.45	8	0.67
Symphony (Unicorn)	57		1	2	1	4	15	4	16	9	5	7	6.18	7	0.53
Winnebago Spectrum	28	3		4	1	2	2		10	5	1	7	5.29	7	1.51
All Responses	719	7	4	17	21	18	53	56	171	147	225	9	7.19	8	0.15

Note: Number of responses required for product to be included in the analysis = 20.

Figure 4
ILS satisfaction in smaller libraries.

Spectrum, a system that has not been actively developed since about 2005, received low marks (5.29). Destiny, the current product from Follett Software Company, geared toward school libraries, did not rank that much higher (6.45) from this group of mostly public library responders. Full-featured systems such as Horizon, Millennium, and Symphony fell in the lower tier of satisfaction scores, presumably due to their complexity relative to the modest needs of these small libraries.

Second, smaller libraries use a different and more diverse set of ILSes: twelve products are used by at least 20 smaller libraries, versus the eight products commonly used by larger libraries. Eight of these twelve are products not used by larger libraries at all.

Many small libraries are public libraries, so we can separate out their responses. Comparing the number of responses for each of the ILS products in figure 5, smaller public libraries, to those in figure 4, smaller libraries overall, we see that public libraries are the majority of those responding from this tier of libraries with smaller collections. Therefore public library satisfaction drives most of the rankings.

On first glance it appears that, as with larger libraries, the overall rankings reflect the public rankings but incorporate additional ILSes used by different library types. However, digging further into the data, nearly all of the ILSes in figure 4 are chiefly used by public libraries; they just do not meet the threshold for inclusion in figure 5. The only exception is OPALS, which is used almost exclusively by school libraries. Therefore, in this survey, the outcome for smaller libraries' ILS satisfaction is chiefly based on public library responses.

Finally, we also examined very large libraries, with collection sizes above one million (figure 6). As with the comparison of larger and smaller libraries, we do see some confirmation that the larger the library, the lower the satisfaction scores given. We might infer that these very large libraries press these systems to the limits, causing problems and gaps in functionality to surface, and impose more difficult support scenarios.

Company Satisfaction

We focus on the question dealing with ILS satisfaction as the core of the survey. As we turn to responses to the other questions, such as that of company satisfaction (figures 7 and 8), we note a very strong correlation (0.81) with ILS satisfaction scores. The survey results do not, for example, reveal any specific cases where libraries hold the product in high regard but do not like the company or its support quality.

As a result of industry consolidation, some companies take responsibility for multiple ILS products: Symphony and Horizon both reside within SirsiDynix;

How satisfied is the library with your current Integrated Library System (ILS)? (collection size < 50,000, public libraries)

Company	Responses	Response Distribution										Satisfaction Score			
		0	1	2	3	4	5	6	7	8	9	Mode	Mean	Median	Std Dev
Apollo	69							1	4	12	52	9	8.67	9	1.08
AGent VERSO	49				1	1	2	2	25	7	11	7	7.33	7	1.29
Library Solution	31				4		2	3	7	8	7	8	6.97	7	1.62
Circulation Plus	21				1	2	2	1	7	3	5	7	6.90	7	1.75
Horizon	22					2	2	5	6	4	3	7	6.77	7	1.28
Millennium	21			1	1	1		2	11	2	3	7	6.71	7	1.75
Symphony (Unicorn)	38			1	1	3	12	1	9	6	5	5	6.29	7	0.81
Winnebago Spectrum	27	3		4	1	2	2		9	5	1	7	5.22	7	1.54
All Responses	465	5	3	9	19	14	39	35	110	93	138	9	7.09	7	0.37

Note: Number of responses required for product to be included in the analysis = 20.

Figure 5
ILS satisfaction in smaller public libraries.

How satisfied is the library with your current Integrated Library System (ILS)? (collection size > 1,000,000)

Company	Responses	Response Distribution										Satisfaction Score			
		0	1	2	3	4	5	6	7	8	9	Mode	Mean	Median	Std Dev
Millennium	60	1	1		1	3	4	5	26	16	3	7	6.72	7	1.03
ALEPH 500	31				3		5	4	14	4	1	7	6.35	7	0.54
Symphony (Unicorn)	27		1		3	1	2	11	5	4		6	5.81	6	1.54
All Responses	174	1	3	2	8	8	20	26	63	31	12	7	6.41	7	0.45

Note: Number of responses required for product to be included in the analysis = 20.

Figure 6
ILS satisfaction in very large libraries.

Ex Libris owns Aleph and Voyager; Follett Software Company offers Destiny as its current flagship product, superseding its legacy products including Winnebago Spectrum, Athena, InfoCentre, and Circulation Plus. In most cases, we did not see large differences among the products supported by the same company, except for Follett Software Company, where Winnebago Spectrum received drastically lower company satisfaction scores than Destiny or Circulation Plus.

Interest in Open Source

As noted in chapter 2, libraries have mixed feelings about open source ILSes. When we break this down by library type and current ILS, we see a more nuanced but still very mixed picture.

If we compare academic libraries' interest in open source (figure 9) to the data on academic libraries'

satisfaction with their current ILS and company (figures 3 and 8), we see a roughly inverse relationship. (Figure 3 excludes smaller libraries, but the picture is quite similar when all are included.) Unsurprisingly, dissatisfaction with the status quo, largely based on proprietary products, correlates with increased interest in open source. Within the Ex Libris fold, libraries using Voyager expressed higher interest (4.30) than those using ALEPH 500 (3.32). For those operating Millennium, academic libraries showed less interest (3.22) than public libraries (3.76).

This increase is slight; average interest in open source is low across the board, with 0 as the most common response. However, the distribution is nothing like a bell curve, or even a straight line. Even though the plurality response is 0, there are as many libraries that answered 8 or 9.

Public libraries (figure 10) have one important difference from academics (figure 9), which is that public

How satisfied is the library overall with the company from which you purchased your current ILS? (public libraries)

Company	Responses	Response Distribution										Satisfaction Score			
		0	1	2	3	4	5	6	7	8	9	Mode	Mean	Median	Std Dev
Apollo	81						1	1	3	10	66	9	8.72	9	1.00
Koha—ByWater Solutions	24								2	9	13	9	8.46	9	1.63
Polaris	88					2	6	3	13	28	36	9	7.90	8	0.85
AGent VERSO	58						4	3	17	12	22	9	7.78	8	1.18
Spydus	22				1		1	5	1	4	10	9	7.59	8	1.07
Circulation Plus	21				1	2	4	5	2	7		9	7.24	7	1.53
Library·Solution	77		1	3	1	4	8	4	17	15	24	9	7.08	8	0.80
Millennium	135	1	1	2	2	5	11	23	37	40	13	8	6.81	7	0.60
Evergreen	40	2	1		1	2	2	7	9	8	8	7	6.58	7	1.11
Symphony (Unicorn)	136	5	4	9	4	11	19	27	27	20	10	6	5.69	6	0.69
Horizon	131	2	3	12	11	14	21	16	33	14	5	7	5.38	6	0.35
Winnebago Spectrum	29	6	2	3	1	3	1	2	2	5	4	0	4.48	4	1.49
All Responses	1,077	22	16	38	27	57	109	117	210	215	266	9	6.71	7	0.24

Note: Number of responses required for product to be included in the analysis = 20.

Figure 7
Satisfaction with company in public libraries.

How satisfied is the library overall with the company from which you purchased your current ILS? (academic libraries)

Company	Responses	Response Distribution										Satisfaction Score			
		0	1	2	3	4	5	6	7	8	9	Mode	Mean	Median	Std Dev
Millennium	182	1	2	7	6	13	14	26	49	42	22	7	6.53	7	0.59
ALEPH 500	74			2	3	8	15	11	24	8	3	7	6.01	6	0.93
Voyager	96		1	3	5	9	12	22	33	11		7	5.93	6	0.71
Symphony (Unicorn)	87	1	3	5	4	12	14	16	18	13	1	7	5.49	6	0.43
Horizon	27	2		3	3	3	4	2	5	4	1	7	5.00	5	0.77
All Responses	578	7	9	25	25	49	65	87	158	103	50	7	6.15	7	0.33

Note: Number of responses required for product to be included in the analysis = 20.

Figure 8
Satisfaction with company in academic libraries.

libraries are much more likely to already be using open source ILSes. For instance, there are several public library consortia that have adopted open source products. (Survey respondents are individual libraries, not consortia, so a single consortial adoption can lead to numerous survey responses.) Of the 47 libraries using Evergreen, all are public; of the 131 using Koha, 56 are public and 30 are academic (the rest represent a wide cross-section of library types). Thirty-nine of 40 Koha libraries who purchase support from ByWater, and 11 of 31 LibLime customers (the plurality), are public libraries.

The higher adoption in open source ILS products by public libraries may have to do with the fact that the functionality in Koha and Evergreen currently fits public libraries better than academics. Both were originally developed for public libraries, though their functionality, and to some degree adoption, has expanded to academic libraries as well.

Those libraries that are already using open source ILSes naturally tend to rate their interest as 9. Aside from that, the overall picture is similar for public and academic libraries. Most public libraries are uninterested, or not very interested, in open source ILSes,

Library Technology Reports   alatechsource.org   May/June 2011

How likely is it that this library would consider implementing an open source ILS? (academic libraries)																
Company	Responses	Response Distribution										Interest Level			
		0	1	2	3	4	5	6	7	8	9	Mode	Mean	Median	Std Dev
Voyager	93	8	9	12	14	6	13	7	7	8	9	3	4.30	4	0.62
Symphony (Unicorn)	87	18	3	11	4	9	9	6	10	8	9	0	4.24	4	0.75
Horizon	27	5	5		2	1	3	5	1	2	3	0	4.07	5	0
ALEPH 500	74	14	13	7	6	7	10	5	5	5	2	0	3.32	3	0.12
Millennium	179	46	18	22	18	8	29	7	14	10	7	0	3.22	3	0.22
All Responses	572	106	58	62	56	33	69	35	45	40	68	0	3.99	4	0.13

Note: Number of responses required for product to be included in the analysis = 20.

Figure 9
Interest in open source systems in academic libraries.

How likely is it that this library would consider implementing an open source ILS? (public libraries)																
Company	Responses	Response Distribution										Interest Level			
		0	1	2	3	4	5	6	7	8	9	Mode	Mean	Median	Std Dev
Koha— ByWater Solutions	24										24	9	9.00	9	1.84
Evergreen	36	1		1		1	2				31	9	8.19	9	0.83
Horizon	128	22	9	15	6	11	16	7	11	11	20	0	4.44	5	0.80
Millennium	135	26	10	25	7	16	13	9	6	6	17	0	3.76	3	0.69
Winnebago Spectrum	27	7	2	3	4	3	2	2			4	0	3.33	3	1.15
Symphony (Unicorn)	134	39	17	11	9	6	19	16	5	4	8	0	3.13	3	0.43
Library· Solution	77	24	6	10	8	2	12	4	3	1	7	0	3.04	2	0.57
Circulation Plus	21	8	2	2		2	6				1	0	2.52	2	0
AGent VERSO	58	14	6	18	3	2	10	4	1			2	2.41	2	0.26
Apollo	78	34	8	7	7	8	9	1			4	0	2.08	1	0
Polaris	88	36	12	17	4	5	5	4	2	1	2	0	1.90	1	0.75
Spydus	22	12	2	2	3	2		1				0	1.32	0	0.64
All Responses	1061	272	100	127	74	76	119	64	36	31	162	0	3.60	3	0.21

Note: Number of responses required for product to be included in the analysis = 20.

Figure 10
Interest in open source systems in public libraries.

with the mode score again 0. However, even when factoring out public libraries already using open source, there is a second peak at 9.

For larger (figure 11) and very large (figure 12) libraries, the picture is similar: low overall interest, with a mode at 0, but a second, smaller peak at 9. Large libraries are much more likely to need functions such as acquisitions, serials control, or reserve book room modules that are not well-developed yet in these open source products—indeed, several comments specifically mentioned the lack of an integrated acquisitions module as a barrier to adoption of open source. However, they may also have more in-house technical knowledge to draw on.

Thus the overall picture in 2010 is of low, even zero, interest in open source, but with a notable and diverse population of highly interested libraries. How has this picture changed over time? Figure 13 shows the percent of respondents expressing any given level of interest in open source products from 2007 through 2010.

Examined this way, we see a polarizing of interest: slightly more libraries have 0 interest, substantially more libraries have maximum interest, and there are fewer libraries at almost every interest level in between. This picture, however, may be slightly misleading, as it includes libraries that have adopted open source ILSes, nearly all of which have very high interest. Figure 14 shows what happens when those

How likely is it that this library would consider implementing an open source ILS? (collection size > 50,000)																
Company	Responses	Response Distribution										Interest Level			
		0	1	2	3	4	5	6	7	8	9	Mode	Mean	Median	Std Dev
Horizon	133	26	7	10	6	13	15	13	9	13	21	0	4.56	5	0.52
Voyager	90	8	11	14	11	6	12	7	6	6	9	2	4.10	4	0.53
Millennium	260	49	24	40	25	16	33	18	20	13	22	0	3.68	3	0.19
Symphony (Unicorn)	165	39	15	18	12	11	20	16	12	5	17	0	3.66	3	0
Library Solution	51	9	5	9	6	3	8	3	2		6	0	3.51	3	0.70
ALEPH 500	86	12	15	10	9	7	14	7	5	5	2	1	3.43	3	0.11
Polaris	66	30	9	7	5	4	4	3	2	1	1	0	1.86	1	0.86
All Responses	1,031	200	106	119	87	65	114	78	64	49	149	0	3.96	4	0.22

Note: Number of responses required for product to be included in the analysis = 20.

Figure 11
Interest in open source systems in larger libraries.

How likely is it that this library would consider implementing an open source ILS? (collection size > 500,000)																
Company	Responses	Response Distribution										Interest Level			
		0	1	2	3	4	5	6	7	8	9	Mode	Mean	Median	Std Dev
Horizon	33	3		3		4	3	5	3	1	11	9	5.91	6	1.04
Voyager	34	2	4	5	5	3	3	3	1	3	5	2	4.41	4	0.17
Millennium	88	10	10	17	8	3	12	8	9	2	9	2	3.95	3	0.85
Symphony (Unicorn)	49	11	4	7	5	3	6	4	2		7	0	3.59	3	0.71
ALEPH 500	40	7	8	6	3	2	5	5	1	2	1	1	3.10	2	1.26
All Responses	1,031	200	106	119	87	65	114	78	64	49	149	0	3.96	4	0.22

Note: Number of responses required for product to be included in the analysis = 20.

Figure 12
Interest in open source systems in very large libraries.

libraries are removed from the sample.

This view amplifies the concerns of the nonadopters; the 0 peak is growing much faster in this view, and the 9 peak more slowly. There is clearly a modest, and modestly growing, interest in open source among people who have not yet adopted it; the increased interest does not solely represent the passion of early adopters. However, once we factor those early adopters out of the picture, the growth in the population strongly uninterested in open source is much more pronounced than the growth in those strongly interested.

Of course, there is a difference between interest and adoption. Do these strongly interested libraries represent future open source users? And are strongly uninterested libraries guaranteed to stick with a proprietary ILS? To investigate this question, we compared libraries' level of open source interest in 2007 against the same libraries' ILS products in 2010. Figure 15 shows what percent of libraries above each interest level in 2007 were using Koha, Evergreen, or OPALS in 2010.

In short, open source interest seems to be predictive of open source adoption. Under 10% of the libraries in this sample (that is, libraries that answered the survey in both 2007 and 2010) are now using open source products—but a third of the most interested libraries are, and likelihood of adoption rises steadily with interest.

Interest is, however, not a guarantee. Even some of the profoundly uninterested libraries have gone open source, and two-thirds of the most interested libraries have not. Investigating these libraries' comments suggests their reasoning. Uninterested libraries may have been pushed to migrate as part of a consortium, jumped ship from a discontinued product, or faced severe cost constraints; some of these libraries became steadily more interested in open source from 2007 to 2010. Interested libraries that did not migrate cite the cost or difficulty of migration, concerns about viability, lack of interest among consortial partners, or lack of in-house technical knowledge. (Similarly, high-interest libraries that did make

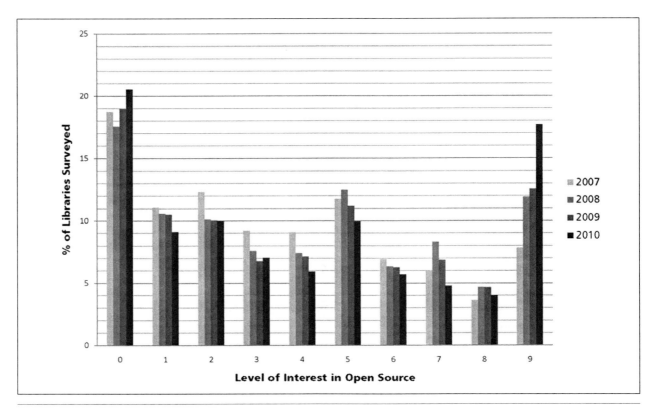

Figure 13
Level of interest in open source systems over time (all libraries).

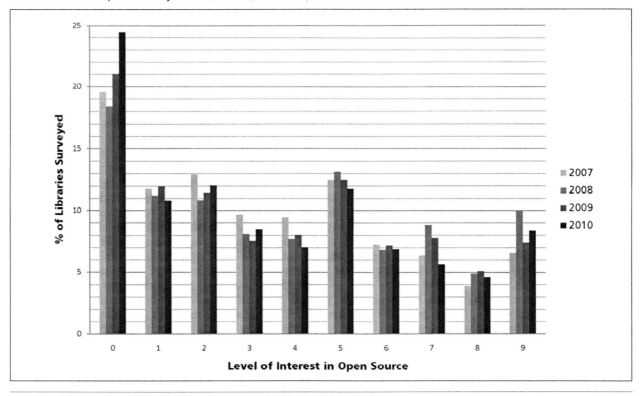

Figure 14
Level of interest in open source systems over time (open source nonadopters).

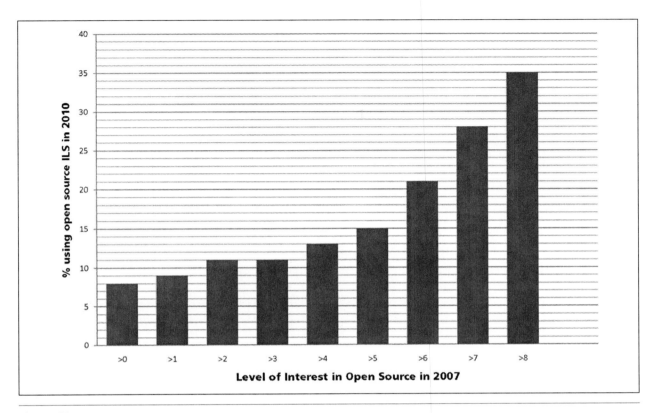

Figure 15
Open source interest versus adoption.

the switch sometimes refer to high levels of in-house technical knowledge.)

To summarize, the overall picture of open source interest is conflicted, and data can be found to support (or undermine) many hypotheses. One might look at the low average interest in open source, and the high number of respondents expressing zero interest, and conclude that these products will not be broadly adopted. One could look at the increasing levels of high interest in open source products, coupled with the elevated likelihood that highly interested libraries will switch to open source, and conclude that we are at the threshold of an explosion—or, considering the comments and the impact of libraries that have already gone open source, conclude that interested libraries with high technical knowledge have already switched, and the rest may be frustrated. Indeed, the same question might appear to have different answers depending on whether one looks at means, modes, medians, or distributions; 2010 alone, or trends over time. Readers are cautioned against drawing conclusions beyond the scope of the data.

Company Loyalty and Migration

The survey asked libraries both their degree of company loyalty and whether they were shopping for a new

ILS. Figure 19 shows the percent of libraries expressing each level of company loyalty that are also shopping for a new ILS. We see, unsurprisingly, that there is a strong negative correlation between loyalty and shopping; libraries that feel strongly disloyal to their current ILS vendor are highly likely to shop around, and libraries with high loyalty are seldom inclined to shop. However, scores run the gamut, and there are 37 libraries that expressed maximum loyalty to their current vendor but are still shopping. How can this be?

If we look more deeply into the data, we discover differences between the low-loyalty and high-loyalty libraries that are shopping. Among the 94 libraries with loyalty 0, 61 are considering open source, either as one of several options or as their only contender; given the overall levels of open source interest discussed above, this is staggering. By contrast, of the 37 libraries expressing loyalty 9, 21 are considering migration to a newer product line from the same company (often as the sole product under consideration), and only 6 are considering open source (one of which has elected to remain with its current, proprietary, vendor). Many of these libraries are using products no longer under development, which seems to be a key factor motivating them to shop despite high loyalty. A few belong to consortia that are considering migrations; thus their high loyalty may not be a factor as decisions are made for the consortium as a whole.

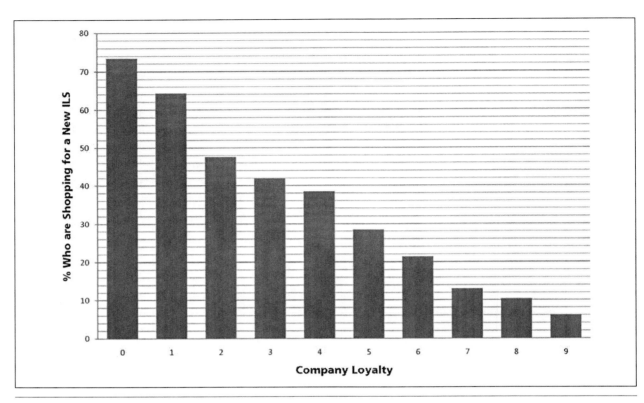

Figure 16
Percentage of libraries shopping for a new ILS versus company loyalty.

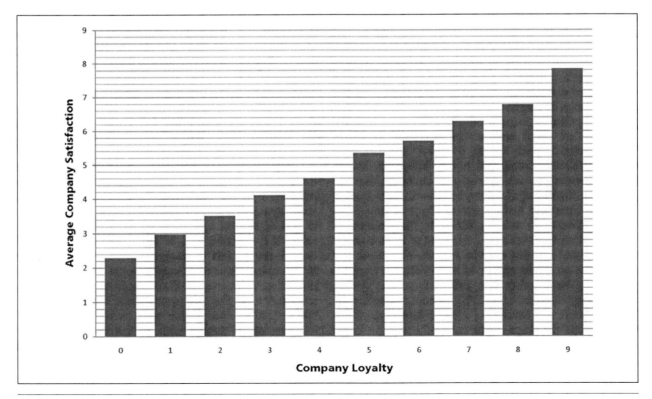

Figure 17
Average company satisfaction versus loyalty.

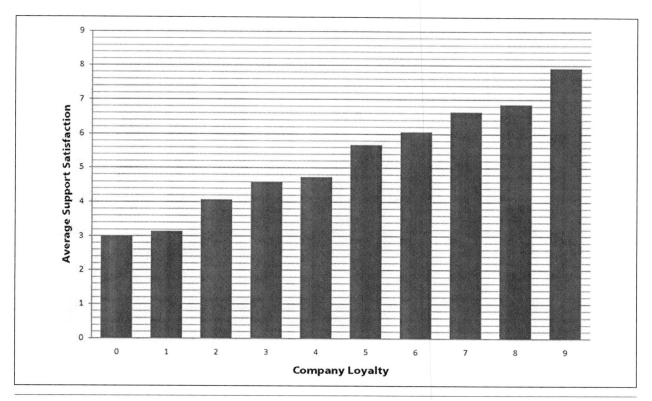

Figure 18
Average satisfaction with support versus loyalty.

We also see systematic differences in company, support, and ILS satisfaction among libraries that are shopping for a new ILS, depending on their level of company loyalty. These are summarized in figures 17, 18, and 19.

We also wondered whether respondents that indicated that they were planning to migrate to a new system actually followed through on such plans. As the Perceptions survey has now been conducted for four years, it possible to investigate this question by making comparisons between the survey data and migrations documented in lib-web-cats.

Of the libraries that responded to the 2007 Perceptions survey, 269 have since migrated to a new ILS. Of these libraries, 176 indicated on their 2007 survey response that they were shopping for a new ILS; 88 that migrated since 2007 did not, at that time, indicate that they were planning for a new ILS. For context, 425 total libraries indicated in 2007 that they were considering a new ILS, and 1,334 said they were not; that is, 41% of libraries that indicated in 2007 that they were shopping have migrated, compared to 7% of libraries that said they were not. These percentages must be taken with a grain of salt. Libraries that were shopping in 2007 and have not migrated may still be considering their options with the intent to migrate in the future. Those which were not shopping in 2007 but have since migrated may have had a very quick migration process

and may have indicated in later surveys that they were shopping. Nonetheless, it seems clear that libraries that say they are shopping for a new ILS have a substantially increased likelihood of acquiring one.

Trends over Time

Average satisfaction level for each of the ten most popular ILSes (figure 20) has remained roughly constant over time. The graphs for average company satisfaction and customer support satisfaction (figures 21 and 22) are similar. For some ILSes there may be slight upward trend, although its magnitude is dwarfed by the variability of the data; it may instead be merely statistical noise.

In comparison with these relatively flat lines, it is interesting to look at company loyalty over time. In Figure 23 we see the percent of libraries expressing each level of company loyalty, 0–9.

There is a dramatic increase in the percent of libraries expressing maximum loyalty to their vendors, along with a modest decrease in very dissatisfied companies. How can it be that libraries are so much more likely to be loyal when their average satisfaction with products and support has not markedly changed?

Two explanations spring to mind. One is money. Many libraries expressed concerns about cost in the

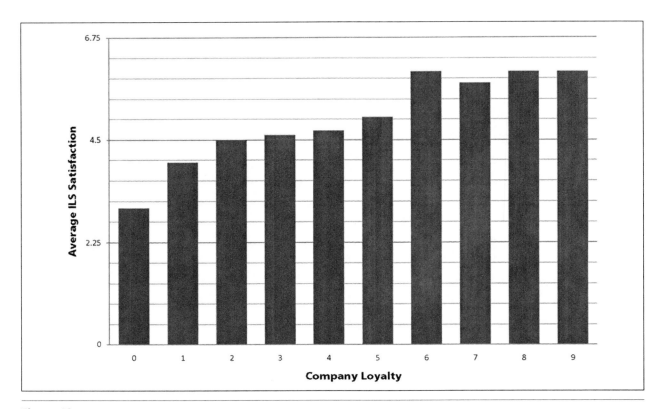

Figure 19
Average satisfaction with ILS versus loyalty.

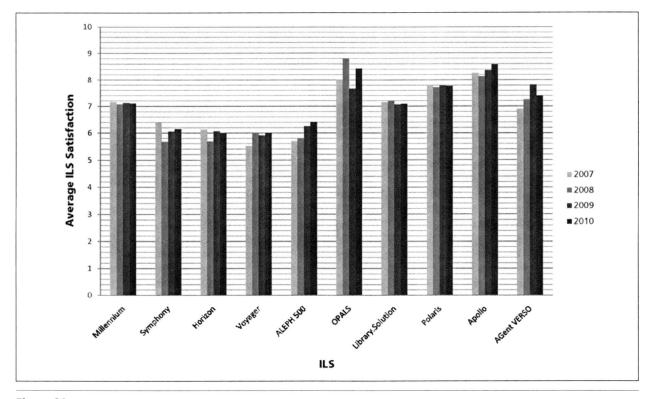

Figure 20
Average level of satisfaction with major ILSes over time.

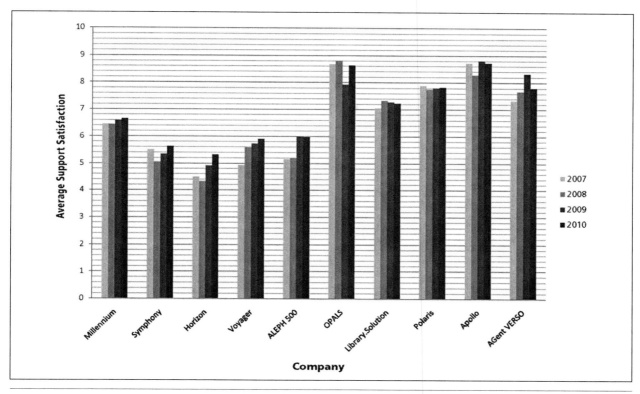

Figure 21
Average satisfaction with company over time.

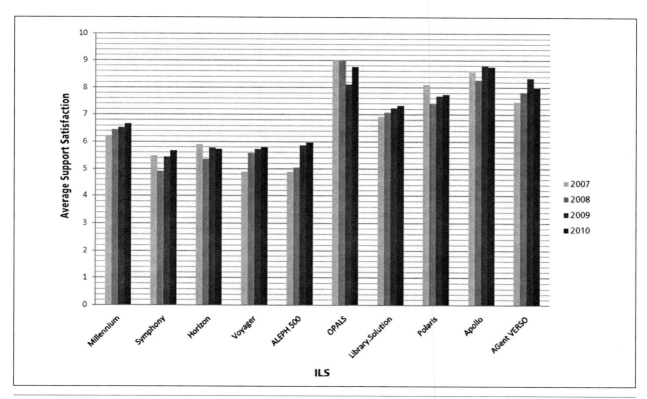

Figure 22
Average satisfaction with customer support over time.

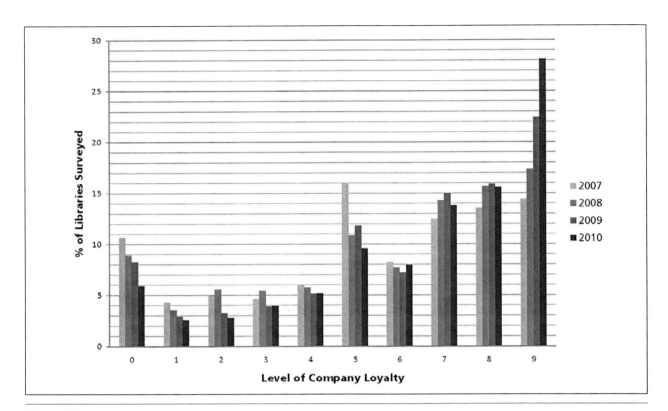

Figure 23
Level of company loyalty over time.

comments, in some cases specifically noting that concerns about cost prevented migration; for instance, "most customers are loath to move to better products due to hassle and cost. The last thing I ever want to do is another system migration!" This concern was especially pronounced for libraries interested in open source (e.g., "Although it is appealing, I doubt that we can afford the programmers to do open source.") And, of course, the economic downturn since 2008 has wreaked widespread havoc on library budgets. However, macroeconomics cannot be the whole explanation since the trend was already evident in 2007–2008. (The Perceptions survey went live in August 2008, when the economy was still strong.)

The second is that libraries have been switching from companies they don't feel loyal to; then, upon adopting a new ILS, they have about the same level of satisfaction as all the other users. In this way, average satisfaction with each product would not change. However, libraries might have much higher loyalty to their new companies, whether because they are optimistic about the reasons they selected it, or because the nightmare of migration is fresh enough in their minds they don't want to think about doing another one.

Indeed, if we examine the libraries that had low loyalty in 2007 (< 3) and high loyalty in 2010 (> 6), we find that the overwhelming majority of them—36 out of 49, 73%—have switched ILSes. (For comparison, among all libraries that responded to both the 2007 and the 2010 survey, only 35% have switched ILSes.)

Unfortunately, of the 13 whose loyalty increased sharply while they remained with the same company, most did not comment, so it is not clear why their feelings changed. (Interestingly, both of the libraries that did comment expressed an interest in open source in 2007, but were unable to make this switch.) Among the libraries that did not comment, the same respondent filled out the survey in nearly all cases, so the difference in loyalty does not reflect a personnel change.

Among those which did switch ILSes, about a quarter were either automating for the first time or abandoning a discontinued product line. Some of the remainder comment on cost concerns or strong dislike of their current ILS. Many, however, do not comment, so (except for libraries abandoning discontinued products) there is no clear reasoning separating libraries whose loyalty increased following a switch, and those whose loyalty increased without one.

Vendor Profiles

Abstract

Chapter 4 examines in depth a few major ILS vendors: proprietary vendors Polaris, Biblionix, SirsiDynix, Innovative; and Koha support companies ByWater and LibLime. These serve a range of library types and span the range of satisfaction ratings. For each vendor, respondents' comments illuminate possible reasons behind the ratings.

As the survey both asks for numerical ratings of satisfaction and provides a free comment field, it is possible to explore the reasons behind libraries' ratings of various vendors. However, readers are cautioned against taking these subjective impressions as definitive. Libraries' experiences with their vendors vary, and every vendor has both satisfied and unsatisfied customers. In addition, there are a few factors that make inferences from comments a challenge.

First, the majority of people who fill out the survey do not leave comments; those who do may not speak for everyone. In fact, it seems likely that people with unusually positive or—especially—negative views are more likely to comment. Therefore, the comments may present an exaggerated view of companies' strengths and weaknesses.

Second, while some issues recur frequently, others may be mentioned only a handful of times. Are they outliers, or do they represent views of the many libraries that did not comment? We have tried to consider how these minority views fit within the general themes for each vendor and quote, or exclude, them responsibly.

Third, many libraries are simply not in a good position to comment in depth, because a consortium or IT office handles contact with their vendor. These libraries typically fill out the numerical questions, but their comment fields address only their lack of contact.

Finally, no matter the general trends for each vendor, libraries should make their own decisions based on their individual circumstances. Many ILS products are best suited to a particular niche, and libraries' satisfaction may mostly reflect whether they are in that niche, not the skills of the company or the quality of its software. Also, libraries' overall satisfaction with customer support sometimes appears to have much more to do with the representatives assigned to their institution than with the company as a whole. Libraries are urged to think about how their specific experiences may vary from the average.

Polaris Library Systems: Polaris

Polaris has earned outstanding ratings for ILS, company, and support satisfaction from 2007 through 2010 (see figure 24). Among commenters, it appears that the major reason for this high satisfaction is an excellent relationship with the company; for instance, the 2008 commenter who said, "Polaris has the best customer service of any company I've dealt with, even outside the library industry." Numerous comments through all four years of the survey compliment the quality and responsiveness of customer service. A few also praise the company for listening and note that its users group is an effective forum for two-way communication; says one 2010 commenter, "A company that listens to their customers wants and needs via the Polaris Users Group enhancement process and does a great job implementing changes that benefit all."

Although there are no areas in which Polaris receives persistently negative comments, libraries do seem to have had mixed experiences in terms of

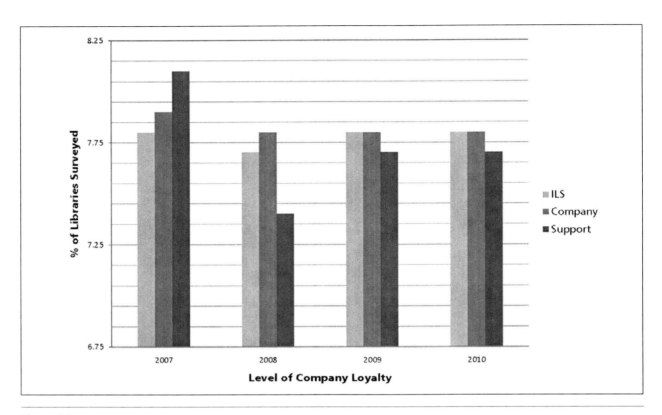

Figure 24
Satisfaction with Polaris over time.

usability and migration. Two commenters refer to the software as "easy to navigate" and "smooth, intuitive," while a third complains of the "hassle" of performing certain searches. Comments on migration note its difficulty and sometimes express dissatisfaction with quality assurance during the process, but typically express satisfaction at the end result. One hurricane-afflicted library liked "their flexibility and willingness to readjust schedules because of our circumstances."

Comments on functionality are harder to interpret. Presumably, given the high ILS satisfaction ratings, most libraries are pleased with Polaris's functionality; however, specific comments on it are most likely to be negative. This may just mean that people are more likely to comment on things that don't work well than on things that do, however. Two academic libraries note that they don't think their demographic is the company's main focus. One 2010 commenter says it is "not the most advanced product out there," but another is pleased that "updates don't cost anything," and several praise Polaris for developing functionality on the basis of listening to users.

One library summarizes this issue as follows: "I like the Polaris company and its philosophy of service. However, we really miss some of the functionality we had on [previous vendor's system]. That being said, there was NO WAY I felt we could continue a relationship with [previous vendor]." Overall, it seems that some libraries are wholly satisfied with Polaris's functionality, and others are willing to make tradeoffs in this area in order to receive superlative customer service.

Biblionix: Apollo

Biblionix's ratings for ILS satisfaction, company satisfaction, and customer support satisfaction (see figure 25) have been consistently outstanding—all average above 8 for all four years of the survey. The comments throughout this period also paint a consistent picture. Commenters note that Apollo is very well-suited to the needs of small and mid-sized public libraries.

Libraries comment favorably on the software. Several note that it is easy to use, and this has been particularly helpful for training volunteers. Others are pleased with the system's flexibility, including a variety of reporting options. Several mention a responsive and forward-looking development process; for example, "They listen to librarians' needs and then design user-friendly and relevant upgrades with those needs in mind." One extremely satisfied library says, "They integrate new technologies and services before any of our neighbor's systems do, and they make us look trendy to our members."

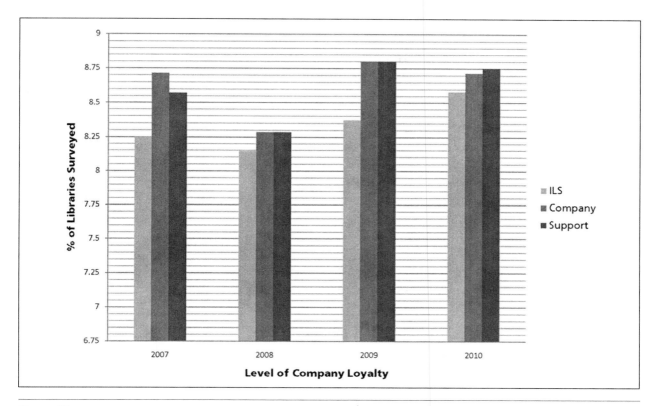

Figure 25
Satisfaction with Biblionix over time.

Where Biblionix truly garners praise, however, is in the area of customer service. Comments like "totally satisfied," "very pleased," and "terrific" are common across all four years of the survey. Libraries specifically praise the company's responsiveness to both feedback and support requests and its speed in addressing issues. Astonishingly, though some new adopters experience the typical stresses of migration, others comment favorably even on this process, due to the quality of support; for example, "Migration was completed overnight, with minimal disruption to staff or customers." Several libraries have comments like "the service is the best I have ever had."

SirsiDynix: Symphony (Unicorn), Horizon, Dynix

As the largest company in the industry, supporting multiple ILS products, SirsiDynix received a large number of responses, many with sharp comments. In 2010, for example, the survey attracted 282 responses from libraries using Symphony, 80 of which provided comments; 185 responses from Horizon with 61 comments; and 13 responses from the legacy Dynix Classic ILS with 6 comments. From these comments a number of themes emerge, many of which address changes in the company, which respondents perceive as producing negative effects on service and product development.

The 2007 survey fell on the heels of acquisition of SirsiDynix by Vista Equity Partners and an announcement that its product development would focus solely on Unicorn, subsequently renamed Symphony. The company has since softened its position on Horizon and continues at least some development. The comments from that first year's survey in 2007 reflected the high level of concern many customers expressed regarding those events. In subsequent surveys, it is of interest to see whether time has healed those wounds and if libraries using Symphony and Horizon have come around to a more positive outlook. In general, while company satisfaction (see figures 26 and 27) seems to have recovered somewhat, the comments have not lost much of their bite; the majority of the comments offered continue to slant toward the negative, though at least a minority reflect strong satisfaction with Symphony and appreciate its maturity and stability. In addition, some Horizon customers, while dismayed that they will eventually have to migrate, like the software they have and appreciate that SirsiDynix has continued to support it. In 2007, at least one response complained that following the merger that the Sirsi and Dynix sides of the company

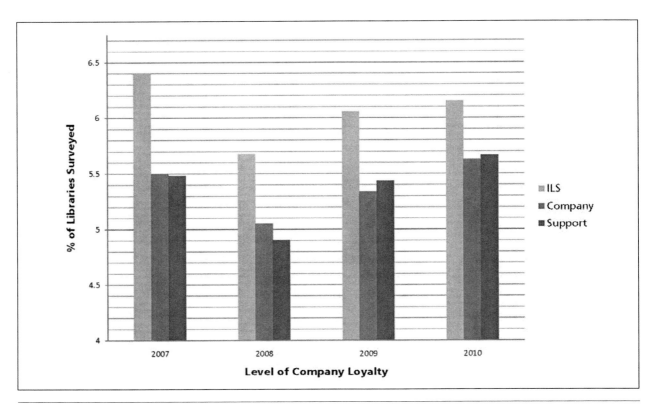

Figure 26
Satisfaction with Symphony (Unicorn) over time.

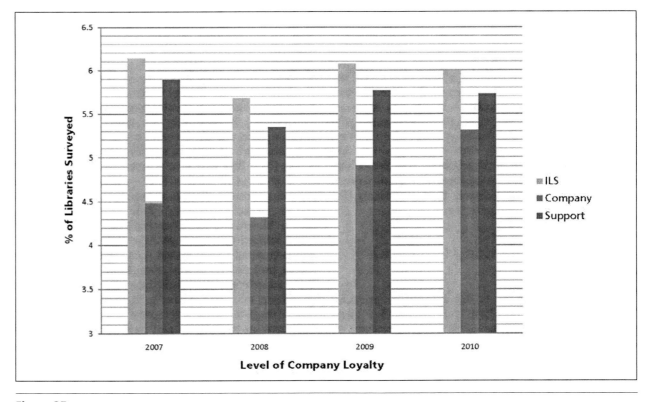

Figure 27
Satisfaction with Horizon over time.

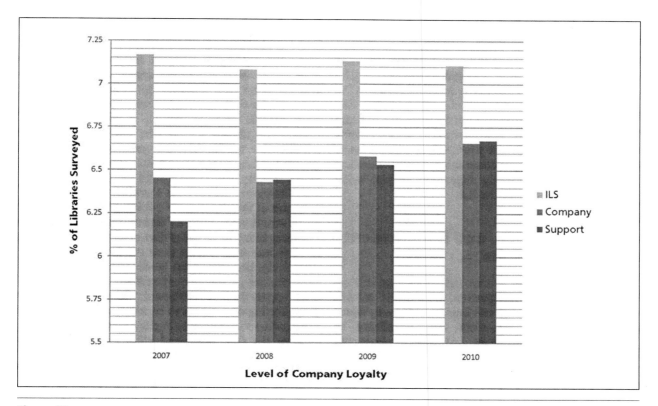

Figure 28
Satisfaction with Millennium over time.

did not communicate well with each other; no such comments appeared in subsequent iterations of the survey following the company's aggressive business integration process.

In 2010, SirsiDynix made further changes in its organization, centralizing support in its Provo facility. This change was implemented to strengthen the company's support capacity. Comments in the latest 2010 survey indicated considerable resistance to this strategy. Criticism was especially strong from international users of both Symphony and Horizon, expressing concern with the loss of local expertise and support options. While some libraries were quite happy with their individual support representatives, others expressed difficulty in locating people with relevant expertise or dissatisfaction with their response time. These concerns about the new support strategy are not reflected in the overall numerical rating for support satisfaction, though, which has not changed in 2010; it may be too early for the effects of this change to be apparent. Again, it will be important to watch survey results in the next year or so to see if this strategy achieves its desired results.

Many comments offered by respondents using SirsiDynix automation products complained about the company's business transitions and impact on product options and direction. A few libraries using Horizon voiced support for the capabilities of that system and concern that they would be shuffled toward Symphony, a product some perceived as inferior. That said, the plurality of migrations away from Dynix and Horizon in 2007–2010 have been to Symphony; it may be that these libraries which are apparently satisfied with SirsiDynix's direction are less likely to comment.

Innovative Interfaces: Millennium

In 2010 the Perceptions survey attracted more responses from libraries using Millennium from Innovative Interfaces than any other automation system. Of the 395 responses received, 110 provided comments. A minority complained about specific problems with Millennium, casting it as clumsy and antiquated, but others called it a solid, modern system and praised aspects of its capabilities and functionality; most seemed pleased with the software. Similarly, some were dissatisfied with support, while others were happy that Innovative worked with them to customize the product around their needs (see figure 28). Overall, satisfaction with the ILS has remained roughly constant from 2007 to 2010, while satisfaction with the company and its support have risen slightly.

The dominant theme of the comments, however, was cost issues. Some mentioned that they did not appreciate the way that pricing was structured, such that any new component was priced separately. The key issue, as revealed by survey comments, lies in the opinion that the costs associated with operating Millennium press the limits of what budgets can tolerate and in the perceptions that alternative arrangements might be less expensive or provide more upgrades as part of the base price. In some cases, this concern has led to libraries considering migrations despite being otherwise satisfied with the ILS.

ByWater, LibLime, and Independent Installations: Koha

Support for the open source ILS Koha provides an interesting point of comparison. Two firms providing hosting and support services for Koha—ByWater Solutions and LibLime—were well-represented in the survey, as were libraries that have implemented Koha independently. Those depending on support from ByWater Solutions gave ILS satisfaction ratings at a very high level (7.86); those using Koha with support from LibLime gave lower ILS satisfaction scores (6.90). Libraries' satisfaction with the ILS may have been linked to their satisfaction with support: 8.44 for ByWater customers and 5.64 for LibLime customers, though one notes support has improved since the acquisition by PTFS. Company satisfaction and support satisfaction were similar for all support strategies (see figure 29).

It's difficult to interpret company satisfaction ratings when a library operates an ILS without support from a commercial company (and, indeed, some commenters noted that these questions did not apply well to them). It may be that the ratings are directed toward its own efforts, toward the broader community of libraries that provide peer support, or to other entities. These independent users rated the ILS as highly as ByWater users (7.87), but their satisfaction with support was lower (7.38).

It should be noted that these are not the only companies providing Koha support; libraries using nine different support companies, as well as independent users and those not specifying a support vendor, participated in the 2010 survey. This is a substantial increase over past years; there were only four support vendors mentioned in 2009, and only one (LibLime) in 2008 and 2007. As there are typically only a handful of respondents in each category, we cannot meaningfully analyze the data. However, it will be interesting to watch the rapid growth in the Koha support market in future years.

Concluding Thoughts

The data represented across the four years of the Perceptions survey provide considerable insight on the dynamics of the library automation industry. As we take the data apart and look at different sectors, each reveals its own distinct issues and concerns. Sifting the results by the size and type of library affords the opportunity to gain a more nuanced understanding of the trends that are not as apparent when looking at the aggregated data.

The survey serves as a barometer to measure the pressure of the industry: the force of library expectations versus what their automation providers deliver. Libraries today have fewer resources to spend on automation and must deliver their services efficiently and effectively. Measuring the levels of satisfaction in the performance of the current systems and the vendors that support them provides useful information to libraries reflecting on whether to continue with their current automation strategy or to explore new tangents.

For the companies and other organizations that provide and support automation systems, the survey provides a source of constructive criticism. The numeric rankings provide a four-year running indicator of the effectiveness of their support programs and whether changes made have produced positive results. The public nature of the results may not feel entirely comfortable—the comments offered by survey respondents include sharply negative statements as well as positive ones. Redacted only to preserve confidentiality, the comments bring to the surface issues and concerns that prevail among library customers and hopefully provide insight to the vendors on what is working and not working about their current product and support offerings. An independent survey such as this one elicits different comments than those that might be offered in response to a company's own efforts to solicit feedback from its customers. Several of the vendors covered in the survey report to the author that their own metrics trend more positively.

Only within the ranks of small libraries do we find superlative satisfaction with their automation scenario. Once we excavate below the surface layer of highly satisfied libraries, we find strata of trends that run in different directions. In this report we have explored some of the differences that arise as we look at public versus academic libraries among those with differing collection sizes. While some companies and products perform better than others, none provide a resoundingly satisfactory solution for most libraries of substantial size and complexity.

The survey seems to reinforce the idea that the costs of the current systems press the limits of what libraries can bear. Of the comments dealing with cost

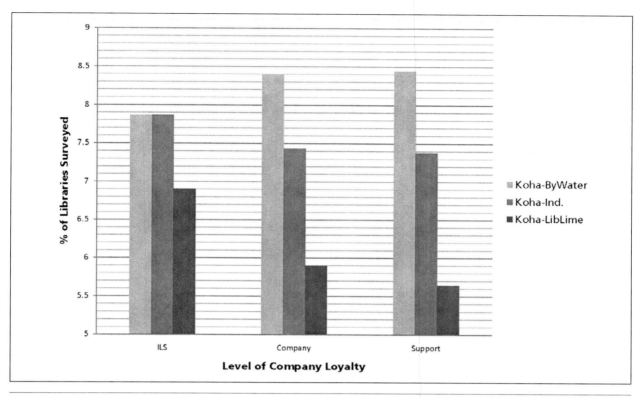

Figure 29
Satisfaction with Koha for major support strategies, 2010.

issues, almost all reflected concern; some state that current costs already exceed what they can tolerate. Hardly any comments reflected a sense that libraries feel they receive excellent value for their investments.

Analysis of the results fails to confirm open source library automation as a panacea. While those already involved with open source continue to support the concept strongly, the survey does not validate the open source ILS as the key to satisfaction. Outside the ranks of those already involved, we detected no evidence of libraries being poised ready to abandon proprietary systems in droves. We saw combinations of open source ILS products and support companies that produced widely varying levels of support and product satisfaction. Companies providing services surrounding an open source ILS face the same kinds of challenges in satisfying their clients as those faced by their counterparts involved in proprietary software.

The four-year view of the survey data both answered and raised questions. In some cases, it confirmed commonsense assumptions: for instance, cost is a major ongoing concern, and libraries with low company loyalty are more likely to migrate away from their current ILS and work with a new vendor. Other trends revealed in the survey results seem more

baffling and warrant further investigation. Given that ILS satisfaction, company satisfaction, and customer support satisfaction have remained more or less constant over the years, why has company loyalty risen so sharply?

The data on the open source market are particularly open to interpretation. Are open source library automation systems nearing the maximum market penetration they can achieve given their reputation for requiring technical skills, or will the rising percentage of highly interested libraries propel them forward? What does it mean for ILS adoption, and the software marketplace, that libraries' interest in open source ILSes is polarizing? As the number of companies supporting open source ILSes rises dramatically, will we increasingly see different entities providing software and support? Given that many open source users commented that the survey did not mirror their situation, will we find ourselves needing to consider what the ILS marketplace means in different terms?

The survey data show that, on average, libraries are moderately—sometimes extremely—satisfied with their software, and fairly loyal to their vendors. However, cost pressures, troubled relationships with vendors, and alternate models such as discovery layers and open source software drive widespread reevaluation; 21 percent of libraries surveyed in 2010 are shopping for a new ILS. While this benchmark stands a bit lower than in the economically stronger years of 2007 and 2008, it predicts that we may be in store for new rounds of churn in the turnover of automation systems. In broadest strokes the survey results do not paint a picture of a libraries in turmoil against their automation systems and vendor. Rather it reflects levels of disconnect between expectation and performance that may drive libraries out of their patterns of inertia and lead vendors toward new models of technology and service with the potential to narrow the gaps of discontent.

Library Technology Reports   alatechsource.org   May/June 2011

34   *Librarians' Assessments of Automation Systems: Survey Results, 2007–2010*   **Marshall Breeding and Andromeda Yelton**

Notes

Library Technology Reports Respond to Your Library's Digital Dilemmas

Eight times per year, *Library Technology Reports* (*LTR*) provides library professionals with insightful elucidation, covering the technology and technological issues the library world grapples with on a daily basis in the information age.

Library Technology Reports 2011, Vol. 47	
January 47:1	**"Web Scale Discovery Services"** by Jason Vaughan
February/March 47:2	**"Libraries and Mobile Services"** by Cody W. Hanson
April 47:3	**"Using WordPress as a Library Content Management System"** by Kyle M. L. Jones and Polly Alida-Farrington
May/June 47:4	**"Librarians' Assessments of Automation Systems: Survey Results, 2007–2010"** by Marshall Breeding and Andromeda Yelton
July 47:5	**"Using Web Analytics in the Library"** by Kate Marek
August/September 47:6	**"Re-thinking the Single Search Box"** by Andrew Nagy
October 47:7	**"The Transforming Public Library Technology Infrastructure"** by ALA Office for Research and Statistics
November/December 47:8	**"RFID In Libraries"** by Lori Bowen-Ayre

ALA TechSource

alatechsource.org

ALA TechSource, a unit of the publishing department of the American Library Association

CPSIA information can be obtained at www.ICGtesting.com
Printed in the USA
LVOW021124101011

249739LV00021B/1/P